Teasing the Tongue

Teasing the Tongue

edited
by
Lorna Crozier

WINTERGREEN
STUDIOS PRESS

Wintergreen Studios Press
Township of South Frontenac
PO Box 75, Yarker, ON, Canada K0K 3N0

Book and cover design by Rena Upitis
Edited by Lorna Crozier and Callista Markotich
Cover photograph by Peter Coffman

Composed in Book Antiqua and Candara, typefaces designed by Monotype Typography and Gary Munch, respectively.

Library and Archives Canada Cataloguing in Publication
Crozier, Lorna.
Teasing the Tongue/Lorna Crozier
ISBN: 978-0-9918722-8-2
1.
Poetry — General.
I. Title. Teasing the Tongue.
Legal Deposit — Library and Archives Canada

Contents

Destined for Miracles   1

Daughter Leaving Home   3

Backpack   4

To my Television   5

Slow Eddie   6

Constable Tobin and the Sow   8

You Are the Absence   10

Silent Bridge Between My Noisy Days   12

To My Parents' Red Fibreglass Canoe, With Love   14

Colourfast   15

To a Lady Susan   17

Ode to A Designer Dress   18

After the animal that drank sound died…   20

Tobias and the Angel   21

A Study in Scarlet Threads   23

These Cabbage Rolls? No, My Mom Didn't Teach
Me To Cook   24

Friend   25

Contributors   27

Destined for Miracles

Leonard Cohen's famous lines "There is a crack in everything / That's how the light gets in" were in the air at this May's poetry session at Wintergreen. We seventeen poets who gathered to listen attentively to one another, to the bird song and to five different species of mating frogs, looked closely at the fractures in our lives, some that seemed small, others so irreparable that it took tremendous courage to "tease the tongue" into speaking. What mended the rifts inside each of us was language. It was a needle "threaded with silk and straw."

"The fragile" and "the tensile" worked together like a spider's string that could be destroyed by a breath. Though it is often television, as one poet reminded us, that is credited with showing "what [is] in the world," in our days together we depended on poetry. Daily it gave us the other side of the news. It highlighted not the political or the rich but the people in our lives who changed us. Take for example the boy Eddie who helped another boy years after the end of their childhood "unlock the doors and head for the light."

We also became acquainted with a sow who wouldn't be restrained, an aunt who nudged an anxious child to be free, a dear elementary school friend who knew "how to stand still" when anger blew through their houses. We looked through a poetic lens at what we usually think of as inanimate: a canoe that teaches a young couple that "we can't/ hold onto everything," a Lazy Susan that defies its name, a designer gown that demands tallness and beauty (not!), and finally, a football-shaped alarm clock, a gift from an uncle who knew his niece "didn't want Barbie crap."

A poet who arrived with a fear of the night came to see the nocturnal Wintergreen woods as "a silent bridge between [her] noisy days." Another found an image to contain the sadness of a dystopian world where animals can make no sound: "loons drowned / of loneliness on stilled lakes." And one writer, using an analogy from painting, captured the sacredness of the hours we chose to work together without speaking: "the pale pure colours of quietude."

What I love and continue to love about poetry was made manifest at Wintergreen. One of the reasons I write and teach is that I continue to believe that saying something on a page can be a redemption of sorts, that "a little dog named Hera, / a fish, / and a little box filled with fish entrails / [can be] destined for miracles."

Lorna Crozier
July 2017

LAURA APOL

Daughter Leaving Home

I love the word *fragile*, love
      the word *tensile* —

and how, in stretching, some things
are both.   Some things

      are not.

Once on Bowen Island,
I saw a spider's web —

      spun silk
    buoyed between branchings,

      shining wet
   with end-of-summer dew —

and tried to fix it
in a photo.   With just the breath
of my approach

it ruined.

      What am I saying, then?

The late fields are yellowing. Here
and there,   a leaf turns.

Each hummingbird
    may be the season's last

— so much distance
    in a sky this blue.

FRANCES BOYLE

Backpack

Dawn moon
without frost
I startle three deer.

Morning coffee
in an orange cup.

Nature sightings at Wintergreen:
one snake four times, those deer
many crows

clouds of blackflies by the doorway
a race to the car.

I always aim to travel light
shoulder my own load
but my backpack is overfull.

Why dangle the possibility
like wires pulled from a circuit box?

Late night swirl of talk
a billow of smoke
today.

Thread the needle
with silk and straw.

MARY LEE BRAGG

To my Television

You are rectangularly calm
in your place above the hearth.
From across the room I summon you.
Tell me what is in the world.

You show me disaster after tragedy
houses tossed in floodwaters
cell phones' shaky pixels
blurred by atomized cement.

Your colour is true, your sound fidelity itself.
You teach me to cook, but not
how to shop for those ingredients.

You lead me into jeopardy
but offer walk-in baths
and stair chairs.

Late at night in your upper channels
the call of love resounds. Its
bouncing simulacrum warms the room
as once the fireplace did.

BRIAN BRITTAIN

Slow Eddie

Much later, Pat next door told me
he used to see you, Eddie,
night loping, daring, darting, giggling,
on down your driveway.
Around about 11, he thought.

Pat said, "We called him *Slow Eddie*, you know."
He couldn't see where you were going.
But Mom and I saw the last bit, Eddie.
We saw you dance, under the new street lamp.
You'd been inside all day. Those were the rules.

Mrs. King said, "Eddie is a mongoloid, you know."
But at night, after strict Dutch parents slept,
you showed us all. No. You shattered us all.
But each one different.

Pat, curious, Mom scared, and me? I don't know.
You helped me see something bigger, something beyond,
I, too, could unlock the doors, head for the light.

You never knew Mom, Eddie. She used to dance.
But later she stopped and just drank.
Mom and I, together with Johnny Carson,
could see your work,
as light and shadows, would bob and flash;
spraying our walls, inside, lighting us up.
"Should be in the *Mental*," Mom said,
"Not out there, all loose and silly."

So, she made the call. They took you away, Eddie.
But, I wanted you to know, that today,
You remind me to get up ...
and go to the light.

SANDRA CAMPBELL

Constable Tobin and the Sow

Oh my! In your splendid uniform! And on this fine spring morning, right here on my doorstep! Yes, this most splendid morning and you! A handsome, strapping man. A sight for sore eyes, I say — and all in the blink of an eye!

Why seems only yesterday — and you, it was you, a mere speck, a tiny freckled thing and oh so sickly — your Mama wringing her hands at Papa's surgery door at all hours of the night. And that mousy squeak that was your voice. That's how we always knew it was you, Freddie.

Do you mind if I call you Freddie?

Time passes yes, yes and in the blink of an eye. Come in! Sit!

Yesterday, was it you I heard? You? A bellowing from way across the Harbour? I have to tell you, Freddie dear, I felt a fright I did and then Sadie saying it was you! Imagine! And on account of my old sow here, my dear Elberta, and that new rule about pigs being tethered and all.

Elberta mind your manners now. Back off!

It's that snout of hers, Freddie, doing what the dear Lord meant it to do — but yes, sometimes in the wrong places — it can happen. You do remember, don't you, once she too was a speck of a thing? Runty pig those others called her, barking their orders at me. Ring her they'd say, or she'll turn your yard into a sea of shit and mud.

Mud they called it — God's good black earth. Why just yesterday — was it only yesterday? All day, she and I, side by side, working that new potato bed.

Turn yourself, Freddie, look out this window here. Her rooting snout upturned all that ground. Imagine our harvest. Can't suppose the root cellar will be large enough…

Now what's this piece of paper you're waving at me? A fine is it? Sadie warned me.

She'll not be tethered, young lad. Not ever.

MARY CORKERY

You Are the Absence

framed on our mantel, regal demeanor
in purple dacron dress, black patent heels
your buyer-for-Simpsons self. Glamourous
Aunt Helen, you jive with our *proper*
selves, sass Dad as he watches wrestling
on TV, set plastic teeth clacking
toward Mom's feet, then float smoke rings
over Christmas dinner.

February, seven kids wait each day
as insulting valentines arrive, one by one
in the mail. On impulse, I slide mine
under the desk, across the aisle, watch
a surge of giggles echo around the room.
Facing the wall in a corner, I smirk —
Aunt Helen the clear winner.

When my other-worldly parents forbid
makeup at thirteen, you wrap
a lavish kit in glitter, disguised as
godmother-birthday-gift. When they stomp
my dream of university, *that haven of atheists,*
you skin them alive
in the kitchen.
I memorize the sharp edge
of your voice as it slices.

Can't imagine you old, Helen. I would still
hold your hand, still talk at you for another
two weeks, two years, two decades
if the hospital hadn't insisted
      I let go.
               I never let go.

Here you are in my turquoise purse
where I harbour
              a wind-up chicken who will arrive
       by mail, to dance the rhumba
           for any girl who needs —
               a nudge, to be free.

SUZANNE DOERGE

Silent Bridge Between My Noisy Days

I will not fear you,
closing in on the path,
consuming this isolated cabin.
It doesn't matter that the way disappears,
and that I am uncertain how to get back.

I have survived other nights —
quickened steps from remote bus stops,
alone — the only one to turn on the light,
creaks on the stairs, intruders on the porch,
unknown animals roam,
the night she didn't come home.
Or that sultry evening, feet on dirt floor,
when they said:
Invading troops gather at the village edge.
I cowered in a secluded room, while they
took up arms, till dawn.
I will not fear you.

Audacious, I stare into your secrets.
Trees take shape…breathe.
Stars persist into my bleakest places.
Merciful illumination reveals only
what we want to be seen:
scratches on the glass disappear.
Somewhere lovers unabashed undress,
fleeing people cross borders,
and a boy is certain his somewhere father
spies the same moon.
Sleep deep.

And when sleep doesn't come, you are a blackboard
across which I screech lists of tasks undone,
erase mistakes, scribble over, try again.
Silent bridge between my noisy days.
I rise to cross you.
Neighbour's blinds pulled, quiet household,
except for the cat's contented snore.
Cup in hand, soft light and verse.

I will not fear you.

SUSAN HALDANE

To My Parents' Red Fibreglass Canoe, With Love

A slant second-hand wedding gift, I suppose. Oh
honeymoon canoe: dry and high
and shifting in your ties
on the roof, you taught us we can't
hold on to everything.

Packed with provisions and slung
overnight between trees you showed us
there are other ways to be
helpful.

Your spine already osteoed, twisting
on our shoulders as we carried you
up rock trails and down,
you taught us sometimes — often —
it's better not to say it.

But plowing prow true
toward the desperate island
while we angled the rain-dark
wall of wind and my husband
said to me   — carefully —
"I'm going to have to ask you
to paddle a little harder,"
and we married our strokes
then, red canoe,
you showed us
our way.

CALLISTA MARKOTICH

Colourfast

Last night I dreamed I was
A watercolour painter.
My careless brushes drowned
Translucent blues, reds, yellows,
Making puddles the colour of mouse.

Today we leave this place
Where we have steeped in colour:
The flaming red of columbine, a canoe
Whose red was cut with faithful love,
Scarlet blood, the crimson gems of pomegranate,
Raphael's wings, red, black and gold,
And rosy cheeks of painted children.
Pale pink designer gown,
Aubergine, luscious, on the cover of a book,
Blue blouse within a sniper's range,
And tawny shades as in a daughter's
Lovely hair, a little fox, the black of sorrow.
Gleam of potted peppers, off-white shade
Of grief, the mellow glaze on cabbage rolls.
The colour of sweat on a young girl's shirt,
Her cry-out for a friend,
Shimmer of streetlight, dancing boy,
Silver rink, Zamboni having passed,
TV's warm flickerings, new-age fire.
The etchy grey as lines dissolve
The map that was not there,
And serene, cool, calla lily white.

But there's a fear, that these hues
On leaving here may blanch or bleed or
Blend and make the colour, mouse.

Tonight I hope I dream
My thirsty brushes drink
The muddy pool into parts,
Precisely, render tinctures
Luminous and clear:
The pale pure colours of quietude
To write contentment, peace and calm,
The brilliants of passion to lavish on
Deepest loves, ferocious hates,
The glows of courage, clarity, wit,
Gold of silence, silver of discourse,
Enduring treasures of this place.

JULIA McARTHUR

To a Lady Susan

That should be your name,
Not a Lazy Susan,
No, not even a Susie-go-round.
Your perfect form, which follows function,
Makes you an icon for the Modernists.
As a revolving sun spreads its light,
You spread your blessing over the table,
A benediction for all diners.

RUTH MCKINNEY

Ode to A Designer Dress

Maybe it was the thirty yards of bias-cut chiffon or the
tiny disks (stitched perfectly into the bodice to reflect light
from candlesticks and silver) that has held us together all
these years.

Last Spring I read a story in the local paper. The designer
had retired and come to live in my small town. I wrote to
her "you don't know me, but I have one of your gowns. I
have kept it for 50 years, and I would love to meet you." (I
enclosed a photo.) I wanted her to know that what she had
created was still valued.

She phoned and said I made her day, invited me to lunch.
When she asked me why I had kept you for so long, I
couldn't find an answer. We talked about our lives, our
travels, but we kept coming back to you. She asked me to
tell her about the closets you had hung in. That took me
back to apartments on Isabella, the flat in Rosedale, my first
Toronto house, and the years we lived together in the big
American house. But I couldn't picture closets. The only
closet I remember is the one I shared with sisters in my
childhood, the one full of hand-me-downs waiting for the
next one of us to grow.

Maybe that was it—you were all mine, and one of a kind. A
designer gown likely imagined for someone much taller
and older and destined for more grandeur. She told me that
the university was creating a collection and they were
looking for her dresses. "Would you ever consider donating
it?" she asked.

Now that you are gone, I have this sense of a loss. Perhaps I have been waiting, all these years to be old enough, or tall enough, or beautiful enough, to be worthy of you.

LISE ROCHEFORT

After the animal that drank sound died... [†]

the world, its altar barren, slept a deep dream
of darkness. dull centuries followed its hollowed
weeping; its mouth, agape, overflowed
with the dry grit of salt. loons drowned

of loneliness on stilled lakes. wolves unclasped
their jaws from the deer's throat, slunk off
and starved to death, knowing that even
the smallest creature held the sacred right

to a last whimper, the largest, a final word.
I would like to tell you that the molten rock
beneath the earth's crust was too far removed
was unaffected. I would like to tell you

that its lava spewed forth and scorched the earth
with cleansing fire, burnt away the long night.
that the storm clouds gathered then, baptized
life into tiny things that stirred and bumped

against each other: that they felt the quiet thrill
of closeness, the semaphore in the moth's wings,
the secret language in the blue chimera
of chemical code that seeks to replicate itself.

do not ask me all these many things I do
not know. but you are welcome to sit by me
now, in silence. to place salt on our tongues
and wait. something will come to us.

---

† After a line by William Stafford.

KATHARINE SMITHRIM

Tobias and the Angel [‡]

If I were an angel
I would want wings like Azarius
who, by the way,
was the archangel Raphael in disguise
in the old, old story
of Tobias and the Angel.

No diaphanous white wings for me.

I want medieval red passion,
black mystery and
gold wisdom.

Then, like Raphael,
I would cast out a maiden's demons,
and restore sight to her father.

Muslims, Jews, Christians
and non-believers alike
would call on me
to protect travellers on their way.

[‡] After the painting *Tobias and the Angel*, 15 c., attributed to the workshop of Andrea del Verrochio.

And many families,
as they did in those times
when a son returned safely from a long journey
would ask a famous artist
to paint me, Raphael,
walking with their son as Tobias,
a little dog named Hera,
a fish,
and a little metal box filled with fish entrails
destined for miracles.

CAROL A. STEPHEN

A Study in Scarlet Threads §

To cut around its crown, to slice slowly
along the ridges of its skin, to gently pull

the two halves open to the tiny jewels,
the deep cinnabar, its red heart.

Pomegranate, painted with such precision,
blood-toned juices pool crimson on a base of foil.

My lips purse, anticipate the sweet-tart taste. My tongue
remembers astringence, the tiny seeds, their bitter white.

So perfect the artist's rendering. I reach out to
dip my fingers in the nectar, but I touch

only canvas ridge and crevice. Only a painted image,
yet so real to fool the eye, to tease the tongue.

_____

§ After a painting by Mary Pratt.

KATHERINE THOMPSON

These Cabbage Rolls? No, My Mom Didn't Teach Me To Cook

When I was a kid I started doing the grocery shopping, once a week after school my aunt Deb would pick me up and take me to the store. Mom was hardly home. Sometimes working, yeah, sometimes drinking, mostly fucked off somewheres with a boyfriend. She wasn't diagnosed then. My sister and me come home from school one day and she's drug all the stuff out of our bedrooms, half on the back lawn in a burn pile, and out front she's got a garage sale going, selling the rest of our shit. She's like "I'm cleaning up." "That's Our Stuff! We. Live. Here. Too!" I had this football shaped alarm clock from the uncle who knew I didn't want Barbie crap. He's not much older than me, but when I was little he seemed way older. I saw it in his house one day and he just gave it to me when I said it was cool. So, I haggled with this man from down the street over my football shaped alarm clock. The mans like "I just bought this", I'm like "That's Mine. We Give Refunds." I figured if I was doing the groceries and cooking I should be able to cook what I wanted. I'd watch cooking shows and try and do what they did on tv, but using what I had, but I wasn't that good at planning. It didn't always work out. Tried making chicken parm with ketchup and Kraft sprinkle parmesan on a fryer bird. I can make chicken parm now, but I couldn't when I was 12.

SUSAN WISMER

Friend

Just turned fourteen.
New school. First day.
Dark circles in the armpits
of my cotton shirt. Elbows
clamped to my ribs. Other kids laughed,
ate burgers and chips from the cafeteria,
while I stared
at my home-made backpack-flattened
egg salad sandwich.

You asked me my name. I had
a friend.

We talked about almost everything,
about brothers and sisters who disappeared
when it was time to do dishes, boys who might
like us or not, girls who whispered
mean secrets.

Not much about fathers. But I could bring you
home. When
anger blew through our houses, we both knew
how to stand still.

You wanted to be an astronaut. You wanted
to learn Russian. My dream was
do well in high school, get a scholarship,
move away.

You moved too. In my address book, so many entries
Vancouver Island, Michigan, California
all those different towns. You joined an ashram,
left, married, had two sons, started a business,
another and another. For years we wrote
letters while our children grew.
_ After your husband left, you wrote.
I only understand now
How you must have felt,
I have never known such pain.

On the day when you phoned, I had
not seen you for nearly thirty years.
Come soon, you said, come—
breast cancer, again.

I did.

Contributors

Laura Apol lives in Michigan, a state she considers to be part of Lower Canada. Wintergreen is her writing home-away-from-home, and the Wintergreen friends she has made over the years have become part of her family-of-the-heart.

Frances Boyle is the author of the poetry collection *Light-carved Passages* (BuschekBooks). Her poems and short stories have appeared in literary magazines and anthologies throughout Canada and in the U.S. Awards she's received include The Great Canadian Literary Hunt, the Diana Brebner Prize, and the Tree Reading Series chapbook contest.

Mary Lee Bragg lives in Ottawa. Her poetry and short fiction has been published in *Ascent, Grain*, the *Windsor Review, Queen's Quarterly,* and ezines in Canada and the US. She has published a novel (*Shooting Angels*, 2004) and two chapbooks of poetry (*How Women Work*, 2010, and *Winter Music*, 2013).

Brian Brittain is a 67-year-old man, an active leadership development consultant and executive coach, working out of Toronto. Happily married to Elizabeth, with two adult daughters and a grand-daughter. Poetry is a new adventure for him, as is spending a week, as the lone guy, with 16 extremely accomplished women.

Sandra Campbell writes fiction and non-fiction and has tried her hand at a few docs. She treasures her Wintergreen retreats with Lorna whose words and ways open her to the deep mystery of trying to express the ineffable in words.

Mary Corkery's first poetry collection, *Simultaneous Windows*, was published by Inanna in 2017. Her poems have appeared in *The Malahat Review*, *The Antigonish Review*, *Room*, *Descant*, and other journals in Canada and beyond. Mary's career has been in social justice and international development. She lives in Toronto.

Suzanne Doerge, originally from rural Illinois, lived in Nicaragua during the 1980s. In recent years, she has served as Director of City for All Women Initiative in Ottawa where she has lived with her partner, Joe Gunn and two children, Benjamin and Daniela. Her poetry has been published in *Liaison*.

Susan Haldane lives in Chisholm Township in Northeastern Ontario. She was blessed and blissed to have another glorious week at Wintergreen, living like a hobbit and learning in the company of the poets.

Callista Markotich is a retired Superintendent of Education, who, in that capacity has written plenty of reports, memos and letters, and knows the power of the written word to inform, influence, request, and thank. Wintergreen, with Lorna and the other poets, provided a deep immersion in this most exquisite of forms, Poetry.

Julia McArthur lives and works in Kingston, by the lake. At the Wintergreen Poetry Retreat she enjoys the chance to think differently. Here she is inspired by Lorna's stimulating teaching, Rena's to-do lists, Diane's cooking, and life in the near wild.

Ruth McKinney is a poet living in Kingston, Ontario. A poetry junkie, she has been writing — for love or money — all her life and is thrilled to finally be able to do it just for love.

LM Rochefort is a bilingual writer and portfolio careerist who lives in Ottawa, ON and Val-des-Monts, QC. In 2016 she was Guest Editor for Carleton University's first themed issue of In/Words Magazine, *Refuge(e)*, and has worked for Arc Poetry Magazine as an Associate Poetry Editor for several years. She is a founding member of the Ruby Tuesdays poetry collective.

Katharine Smithrim is a reluctant writer. She would rather sing, walk, read, sew, or swim. Her publications include *Prayers for Women Who Can't Pray* (with Melanie Craig-Hansford, Wintergreen Press), *Listen to their voices: Research and practice in early childhood music* (with Rena Upitis, Canadian Music Educators Association) and *The arts as meaning makers: Integrating literature and the arts throughout the curriculum* (with Claudia Corbett, Prentice Hall).

Carol A. Stephen is a Carleton Place poet. Former member of CAA-NCR and Tree Reading Series boards. She has won awards or been shortlisted in CAA's National Capital Writing Contest and has appeared in anthologies, journals and online. Carol has authored three chapbooks and coauthored two chapbooks of collaborative poems.

Katherine Thompson is from Vancouver Island and resides in Southwestern Ontario.

Susan Wismer is a poet, a gardener, a grandmother, a dancer. She lives gratefully nestled by the shores of Georgian Bay in Collingwood, Ontario.

Wintergreen Studios Press is an independent literary press. It is affiliated with the not-for-profit educational retreat centre, Wintergreen Studios, and supports the work of Wintergreen Studios by publishing works related to education, the arts, and the environment.

www.wintergreenstudios.com

WINTERGREEN
STUDIOS PRESS